# PersonaliTrees

Let the Human Spirit Awaken in the Presence of Trees

# PersonaliTrees

Let the Human Spirit Awaken in the Presence of Trees

Joan Klostermann-Ketels

FINDHORN PRESS

© Joan Klostermann-Ketels 2010

The right of Joan Klostermann-Ketels to be identified as the author
of this work has been asserted by her in accordance with the
Copyright, Designs and Patents Act 1998.

Published in 2010 by Findhorn Press, Scotland

ISBN 978-1-84409-191-1

A CIP record for this title is available from the British Library.

Edited by Nicky Leach
Cover & interior design by Damian Keenan
Photography by Joan Klostermann-Ketels

Printed and bound in China

1 2 3 4 5 6 7 8 9 17 16 15 14 13 12 11 10

Published by
Findhorn Press
305a The Park, Findhorn
Forres IV36 3TE
Scotland, UK

*t*  +44 (0)1309 690582
*f*  +44 (0)131 777 2711
*e*  info@findhornpress.com

www.findhornpress.com

# DEDICATION

PERSONALITREES is dedicated to our beautiful sister, Pat Klostermann-Lahey, who said she never got tired of looking at the magnificent old trees near her home.

If breast cancer hadn't shortened her life, she would probably be walking in the woods, laughing, or climbing the trees in this book!

A most amazing spirit and one of the kindest hearts on the planet. Here's to you, Pat. May your spirit soar always through the treetops and among the stars, where you belong.

# AWAKENING

TREES ARE SPIRITUAL STORYBOOKS. From seedlings to dust they talk to us about the nature of life. We need only take the time to see, feel and listen. Perhaps it is becoming a lost art. These days we move so fast that we hardly notice. It is not surprising. Technology requires that we process and perceive by the second. Trees tell their stories by decades.

Spirits are all around us, particularly as trees. Trees strike human forms. They speak our language. They have faces. They are animated. A message that is there one day may be gone the next. Long after they stop sprouting leaves or needles, they continue to act out their stories. They smile, point, pose and play charades. Sometimes subtle, sometimes raucous, they express every human emotion and condition. They hold each other up, and shelter those who need it. It is with the greatest dignity — and even humor — that they show us the way to live, and die. Even as their limbs fall to the ground, the branches continue to tell their stories if we pay attention and listen.

Ever since my childhood, trees have been a connecting point to the world around me and the essence of life. As do most children, I instinctively understood the spirit energy of trees. One of my favorite trees grew in the pasture by the creek on our family farm. It was where I went whenever I needed to feel safe. It was my refuge.

# AWAKENING

I felt completely wrapped in its spirit and would breathe a sigh of relief with each visit. But as the years went by there was much less time for walks and breathing in the energy and spirit of trees.

In the spring of the year after the one in which I was treated for breast cancer, I took a walk. It didn't start out differently from other walks around the lake. But after a year of slowing down, forced on me as it was, my sleeping spirit shook loose and my eyes were opened once again to the spirit of the trees. The walk took me full circle that day — literally back to my roots — and I once again breathed a sigh of relief as I wrapped myself in their energy. And I began to listen and pay attention once again.

This book is about rediscovering the joy and the mystery of seeing things that are too perfect for coincidence. It is an invitation to experience the essence, presence and spirit energy of the trees around you. I am hopeful that it will help bring families and friends together in spirit as they drive down the road or take walks together.

Breathe them in. Be still and listen to their stories.

# ACKNOWLEDGEMENTS

MY DEEPEST GRATITUDE and thanks go out to Sabine at Findhorn for seeing this project as a worthy venture. And to Thierry, whom I refer to as my angel. He has been my guiding light through the entire process. The staff at Findhorn has been incredible!

Many thanks to John Smith for his time and talent. Let's go fishing again soon! A special note of thanks to my three children. Michelle, Rachel and Matt, you are my heroes. I want to also note that it was Rachel who came up with the title — *PersonaliTrees*!

I can't begin to thank all the friends and family by name who have offered encouragement to follow through on this project. Your unwavering support and conviction that this book needed to be published is truly appreciated. Thank you!

And finally, the most talented and intelligent person I have ever met — the absolute love of my life — my husband, Denton. Without you this book would still be a figment of my imagination. You had the perceptiveness and perseverance to show me what the book might look like. You believed in me from the very start, and I could not have accomplished this without you. Nor would I want to. I can't begin to express the love and respect I have for you. Thank you, boss.

# THE FOUR SEASONS

MANY OF THESE PICTURES show trees in winter or trees that are very ancient. Some may even appear to be at the end of life. The lesson we can learn from this is that trees, like people, show their true characters when the covers and the camouflage have been stripped away, or when age brings us to be most truly our essential selves.

# HAPPY

---

"Now and then it's good to pause in our
pursuit of happiness and just be happy."

— GUILLAUME APOLLINAIRE —

# JOYOUS

---

"The tree which moves some to tears of joy
is in the eyes of others only a green thing
that stands in the way.
Some see nature all ridicule and deformity
and some scarce see nature at all.
But to the eyes of the man of imagination,
nature is imagination itself."

— WILLIAM BLAKE —

# ELATED

———— ·❖· ————

"Find ecstasy in life;
the mere sense of living
is joy enough."

— EMILY DICKINSON —

# ANCHORED

"Be sure you put your
feet in the right place,
then stand firm."

— ABRAHAM LINCOLN —

# SPEECHLESS

"Saying nothing…
sometimes says the most."

— EMILY DICKINSON —

# FLEETING

———◆———

"Be happy for this moment.

This moment is your life."

— OMAR KHAYYAM —

# ENTHUSIASTIC

"There is an eloquence
in true enthusiasm."

— EDGAR ALLAN POE —

# STOIC

***

"Give me a firm place to stand,
and I will move the earth."

— ARCHIMEDES —

# HUMBLE

"If the only prayer you ever say
in your entire life is thank you,
it will be enough."

— MEISTER ECKHART —

# RESILIENT

———◆———

"Perseverance,
secret of all triumphs."

— VICTOR HUGO —

# EVOLVED

"As we grow old,
the beauty steals inward."

— RALPH WALDO EMERSON —

# FEARLESS

---

"Character is like a tree
and reputation like a shadow.
The shadow is what we think of it;
the tree is the real thing."

— ABRAHAM LINCOLN —

# INQUISITIVE

---

"One learns people through the heart,
not the eyes or the intellect."

— MARK TWAIN —

# WEARY

"It is not so much for its beauty that the forest
makes a claim upon men's hearts, as for that subtle
something, that quality of air, that emanation
from old trees, that so wonderfully changes and
renews a weary spirit."

— ROBERT LOUIS STEVENSON —

# DIPLOMATIC

———◆———

"Anybody can become angry –
that is easy, but to be angry with
the right person and to the right degree
and at the right time and for the
right purpose, and in the right way –
that is not within everybody's power
and is not easy."

— ARISTOTLE —

# PERSISTENT

———◆·❖·◆———

"Energy and persistence
conquer all things."

— BENJAMIN FRANKLIN —

# CONFIDENT

---

"Confidence is a plant of
slow growth in an aged heart."

— WILLIAM PITT —

# PLAYFUL

—◆◆◆—

"Live and work
but do not forget to play,
to have fun in life
and really enjoy it."

— EILEEN CADDY —

# WISE

———◦◦◦———

"The art of being wise
is the art of knowing
what to overlook."

— WILLIAM JAMES —

# SPIRITED

"Spirit has fifty times
the strength and staying power
of brawn and muscle."

— MARK TWAIN —

# DEFIANT

———✦———

"Show respect to all people,
but grovel to none."

— TECUMSEH —

# ACHILLES HEEL

"There are two kinds of weakness,
that which breaks and that which bends."

— JAMES RUSSELL LOWELL —

# FLAMBOYANT

⸻

"One arrives at style only with
atrocious effort, with fanatical
and devoted stubbornness."

— GUSTAVE FLAUBERT —

# PROTECTIVE

---

"Happy are those who dare courageously
to defend what they love."

— OVID —

# FRIGHTENED

———— ◆◈◆ ————

"Quiet minds cannot be perplexed
or frightened but go on in fortune
or misfortune at their own private pace,
like a clock during a thunderstorm."

— ROBERT LOUIS STEVENSON —

# LOOPY

"No man is sane who does not know
how to be insane on proper occasions."

— HENRY WARD BEECHER —

# LOVING

"The ordinary acts we practice every day
at home are of more importance to the
soul than their simplicity might suggest."

— THOMAS MOORE —

# NURTURING

———— ◆◆◆ ————

"Let parents then bequeath
to their children not riches
but the spirit of reverence."

— PLATO —

# BALANCED

"Go some distance away because
the work appears smaller and more
of it can be taken in at a glance,
and a lack of harmony or proportion
is more readily seen."

— LEONARDO DA VINCI —

# IRRESPONSIBLE

"You cannot teach a man anything.
You can only help him discover it
within himself."

— GALILEO GALILEI —

# INSEPARABLE

"Humankind has not woven
the web of life.
We are but one thread within it.
Whatever we do to the web,
we do to ourselves.
All things are bound together.
All things connect."

— CHIEF SEATTLE —

# RESOLUTE

—◦◦◦—

"To know what you prefer, instead
of humbly saying Amen to what
the world tells you you ought to prefer,
is to have kept your soul alive."

— ROBERT LOUIS STEVENSON —

# LOYAL

———◦━━◦◦━━◦———

"The measure of a man's real character
is what he would do if he knew he never
would be found out."

— THOMAS B. MACAULAY —

# CHIVALROUS

"If a man be gracious
and courteous to strangers,
it shows he is
a citizen of the world."

— FRANCIS BACON —

# HARMONIOUS

---

"A man's growth is seen in the
successive choirs of his friends."

— RALPH WALDO EMERSON —

# PATIENT

"Have patience.
All things are difficult
before they become easy."

— SAADI —

# VIGILANT

"If you cannot find the truth
right where you are, where else
do you expect to find it?"

— DOGEN —

# REVERENT

---

"When the solution is simple,
God is answering."

— ALBERT EINSTEIN —

# COURAGEOUS

"To be an artist includes much;
one must possess many gifts –
absolute gifts – which have not been
acquired by one's own effort.
And, moreover, to succeed, the artist
must possess the courageous soul."

— KATE CHOPIN —

# WOUNDED

———— ◆•◆•◆ ————

"Everything that happens
happens as it should,
and if you observe carefully,
you will find this to be so."

— MARCUS AURELIUS —

# MYSTICAL

·——◈——·

"We dance around in a ring and suppose,
but the Secret sits in the middle and knows."

— ROBERT FROST —

# FORMIDABLE

———— ◆ ————

"He did each single thing
as if he did nothing else."

— CHARLES DICKENS —

# INSPIRED

—◦◦◦◦◦—

"It always happens that when
a man seizes upon a neglected
and important idea,
people inflamed with the same notion
crop up all around."

— MARK TWAIN —

# HAUNTED

---

"It is as hard to see one's self
as to look backwards
without turning around."

— HENRY DAVID THOREAU —

# MINDFUL

―⟡―

"The outward man is the swinging door;
the inner man is the still hinge."

— MEISTER ECKHART —

# HEARTBROKEN

—◆◆◆—

"Expectation is the root of all heartache."

— WILLIAM SHAKESPEARE —

# GRIEVING

---

"Truly, it is in the darkness that one
finds the light, so when we are in sorrow,
then this light is nearest of all to us."

— MEISTER ECKHART —

# GRACIOUS

"You cannot do a kindness too soon,
for you never know when it will
be too late."

— RALPH WALDO EMERSON —

# UNRAVELING A PARADOX

A tree stands naked in the fall of the year

stripped of everything that once made it

beautiful and majestic

Now barren

With its branches reaching toward the heavens

yearning for the warmth of the sun

hidden behind thick, callused clouds

— a sign of winter nearing

And it wonders why,

when it needs protection most,

there is nothing left

but a tree standing naked

in the fall of the year.

— JOAN KLOSTERMANN-KETELS —

# AFTERWORD

IN AUGUST OF 2009, a violent hail and wind storm decimated parts of the beautiful greenbelt area around Pine Lake in Iowa where many of these pictures were taken. The trees and the messages they conveyed about their lifetimes (and ours) were lost forever, or would have been if they had not been captured in photographs. The sadness was overwhelming as I had come to consider these spirits my friends. I was particularly moved by the disappearance of Fleeting, whom I had also come to know as Running Man.

Our world is indeed fleeting. The importance of seeing and paying attention to our surroundings and the people and things in it was amplified by this natural disaster. But it is nature's way. The spirits are still there and will be expressed in other forms by other trees who will reveal their messages, all in good time.

# FINDHORN PRESS

*Life changing books*

For a complete catalogue,
please contact:

Findhorn Press Ltd
305a The Park, Findhorn
Forres IV36 3TE
Scotland, UK

*t* +44 (0)1309 690582
*f* +44 (0)131 777 2711
*e* info@findhornpress.com

or consult our catalogue online
(with secure order facility) on
www.findhornpress.com

For information on the Findhorn Foundation:
www.findhorn.org